The New Life

Other Books by Richard Tillinghast

The New Life

Poems by Richard Tillinghast

Richard Tillinghast

Copper Beech Press
Providence

Grateful acknowledgment is made to the editors of the following journals, in the pages of which many of these poems originally appeared: *AGNI, Bear River Review, Cork Literary Review, Cortland Review, Five Points, The Georgia Review, Gettysburg Review, Harvard Review, Hudson Review, Hunger Mountain Review, Irish Pages, Margie, Michigan Quarterly Review, The New Criterion, The New Republic, Ploughshares, Poetry in Performance, Poetry Ireland Review, Poetry London,* and *Southern Review.*

"Glimpse of a Traveller" was published in the anthology *Blues for Bill;* "Big Doors" was featured on *Poetry Daily;* "They Gambled for Your Clothes" and "Arrival" were among a group of poems awarded the James Dickey Prize by *Five Points* magazine in 2006; "What the Gypsy Woman Told Me" is included in *Poetry Calendar 2007: 365 Classic and Contemporary Poems,* Alhambra Publishing; and "In the Parking Lot of the Muffler Shop" is included in *The Best of Irish Poetry 2007.*

Lines seven and eight in the second stanza of "A Love Story" are borrowed from "The Barroom Girls" by Gillian Welsh.

For information, address the publisher:
Copper Beech Press
Post Office Box 2578
Providence, Rhode Island 02906

Library of Congress Cataloguing-in-Publication Data

Tillinghast, Richard.
  The new life : poems / by Richard Tillinghast. — 1st ed.
    p. cm.
  ISBN-13: 978-0-914278-83-2 (alk. paper)
  ISBN-10: 0-914278-83-5 (alk. paper)
  I. Title.

PS3570.I38N49 2008
811'.54—dc22

2008002041

Set in Georgia by Sans Serif
Printed and bound by McNaughton & Gunn
Manufactured in the United States of America
First Edition

to Grace

nil difficile amanti

Contents

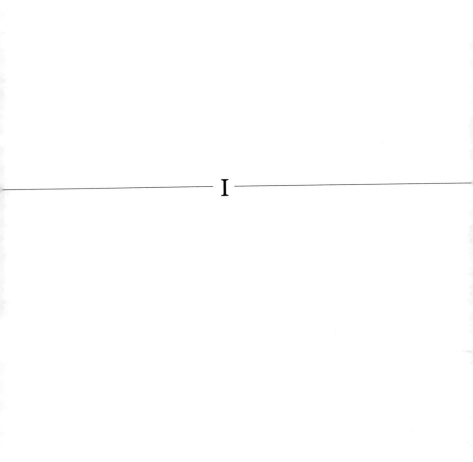

I

The New Life

dawns obscurely one morning
as you wake.
Pale light
gives a lick of white
to the woodwork framing a north-facing window.

It begins as imperceptibly
as the sound of a fountain pen
filling with fresh ink.

The new life
means deciding to leave,
shaving your head,
putting your things into two shopping bags
and getting on a bus.

The bare spot on your ring finger
reddens in the sun.

In the new life you wake up under a bridge
and light two cigarettes
off a single match—
one for your companion,
one for yourself.

There Is a Room I Never Go Into

There is a room I never go into.
There is a sound I dread to hear—
the sound the wind makes in the trees
and the doors it slams shut
as it brings autumn in.
I know I won't see you when the days darken,
when the dryness that's in the leaves this afternoon
becomes all there is.

I never go into that room anymore.
The furniture would look up at me in alarm
if it saw me coming in.

A novel I read there once—
Russian or Irish from the last century—
streams into my mind.
Children from that book
come into the world as if by accident.
Rough exchanges and betrayals, strange
bedfellows in a mahogany bed.
A window blows open to a thunderstorm.

Doors slam, a woman smashes five
cut-glass wineglasses, one after the other,
wedding presents, against the kitchen wall
and cuts her hands.
A house burns, horses pound
their hooves against the stable doors
while down in the valley below, a river
runs blackly through.

I shiver at the sound the wind makes
in the beech trees at the edge of the property,
airy and smooth
as my skin feels after soap and water.
Birds sing a song I know but can't place—
swallows perhaps,
who won't be here in the months when the days darken.
Neither your hand nor mine
will reach up to switch on the light at four o'clock.

The tires of the taxi coming to get me
grind the driveway gravel
as the tide does going out.
My fingers go cold.

The children with their fears,
the world's rough handling of them.
That furniture like the furniture at a funeral.
The sound of breaking glass,
the woman with blood on her cut fingers
staining the white handkerchief she has tied around
    them.
The cold in my own fingers today.

I must find room for all of that
in the chambers of my heart.
There is a room,
and a door beyond doors that open and close,
like a tide that goes in and out,
that cleanses and heals.

Meeting on the Turret Stairs

"Lie down beside me," I whispered.
So we lay on the bed
in that room that was the whole world to us.
Outside, the innkeeper's children
kicked a soccer ball along the quay.
Seagulls flocked and dispersed,
and the busy foolish world went about its foolish
     business.

I shut my eyes and
we met on turret stairs.
I felt the braid of your hair
brush my cheek like a glance.
In the distance someone was blowing a horn.
Voices, and boots hurrying across the boards overhead
as the tower awoke by torchlight.

I opened my eyes then and saw
you watching me from the pillow,
your agate eyes two demi-lunettes.
Horses neighed in the place I was coming out of,
and stamped their iron-shod hooves
on the stones of the stable yard below,
striking sparks like the flinty stars.
A banner snapped in the sharp breeze
as dawn blazed through.
I could smell a river close by,
your body opening to my hands.

Dust Motes

The light turned from tawny to golden,
lion's mane to gold-letter illumination
as we passed our afternoon in bed.
A flotilla of dust motes drifted
unanchored through our sunset window.

The old word *courtship* suited us, and the days we
    courted
were becoming legendary to us
as stories of the Grail were
to pilgrims who read their lines in Latin
by the light of a tallow candle
guttering on a ledge chiseled from limestone.

Those chronicles
glanced back and forth from your eyes to mine
and took us back to our first afternoon,
when we walked uphill through an avenue of hazels
a little out of breath and unsure.
Our hands hadn't found each other yet,
but our thoughts had.

Months later, as we sheltered in the ruin
of a roofless old church,
we found the stone coat of arms whose motto
we took as our own:
Nil difficile amanti.
A lion propped it up with stone paws,
and rain made those letters glisten.

Let there be a monk, a kindly man of our imagining.
Seat him in a scriptorium love fashions stone by stone.
Kindle a fire to keep his fingers nimble
as he dips his brush
cut from a unicorn's mane

into a pot of Byzantine gold
brought back by Crusaders.
Let him write in ink mixed with rainwater
our legend
so you can read it to me
as we lie in bed in the afternoon.

From *La Vita Nuova*, II

from the Italian of Dante

Nine times the heaven of light had wheeled round in its rotation to the point where it had been at my birth, when there first appeared to my eyes the resplendent lady of my mind who was called Beatrice by many who do not know what it means to call her that.

She had been in this life for the length of time it took the heaven of fixed stars to move toward the east by the twelfth part of one degree; so that she came to my sight almost at the beginning of her ninth year, and I saw her just about at the end of my ninth. She appeared dressed in the noblest of colors, a frank and unpretentious crimson, belted and ornamented in a manner that suited her young age.

At that moment I say in all truth that the spirit of life, which occupies the most secret chamber of the heart, began to convulse so violently that the smallest pulsations of it were excruciating; and while it trembled it spoke these words: *Behold a god stronger than I, who comes to rule me.*

Then the animal spirit, which inhabits the high chamber where all the spirits that govern the senses carry their perceptions, began to be filled with amazement and, conversing directly with the spirits of vision, spoke the following words: *Now is the source of your blessedness revealed.*

And at that moment the natural spirit, which sits in the place where our nourishment is digested, began to weep, and weeping spoke these words: *Oh misery! From now on I will often be impeded.*

From that point I tell you that Love held sovereignty over my soul, which became subject to him, and he began to acquire such confidence and mastery over me through the power my imagination granted him, that he obliged me to do everything to please him.

Many times he ordered me to go out and seek occasions to see this angelic child, so that often while I was still a boy I went in search of her and saw that her bearing was dignified and worthy of praise.

And even though her image, which was always with me, emboldened Love to hold sway over me, yet there was such a nobility in its power that at no time did it allow Love to rule me without the faithful counsel of reason in those things where such counsel was useful to hear. . . .

What the Gypsy Woman Told Me

You will grow up to be
a restless man with cold hands
            and a hard-to-reach heart,
      the gypsy woman told me
                  as she opened my palm.
I was seventeen then, my hands unmapped,
            my heart as inaccessible as Tibet.

      A soap opera played soundlessly on the TV
            in her little trailer parked in a muddy field
at the edge of a fairgrounds
            on the outskirts of a Southern city.
      She took some of the dollar bills I made from
      playing drums
                  in a band at the county fair
      and tucked them into her patent-leather purse.

      Our first night together
                  I thought of that gypsy
with her blackened fingernails
      and her trailer that smelled of camphor and
      patchouli—
the night we sat in your car by the sea in August
            with the windows rolled down
                  and watched for shooting stars.
      The night you laid your head in my lap
            and told me your story and I told you mine.

Open your hand, I can hear her saying.
            That's your heart line here,
                  and this is your life line.
      She stabs my palm with her blunt finger.
See where it stops and spreads like a stream gone
underground?
            Here it surfaces like a spring or holy well.

We found that well today, you and I,
    miles hiked, boots muddy,
        halfway up a mountain.
    Pilgrims, travellers and settled folk
      had torn off strips of cloth
and tied them to the whitethorn branches with wishes and
    prayers,
    leaving as offerings cheap rings and lockets,
      Polaroid shots of babies,
        a pocket knife, a lipstick.

We cupped our hands and drank.
        We plunged our faces into that clarity,
seeing the map of our future shimmer in the ripples
      where the surface of the pool was a skyful
        of rain striking a skylight:
    the stones of an old tower destroyed and rebuilt,
red rowanberries on a storm-struck tree outside our
    window,
    ourselves in a walled garden to which we had found
    the key,
      the warmth of your fingers mapping the lines
of my palm.

When your face rose clearly from that dreamy pool
        I knew I was where I was going.

      I turned back through the years
and gave the gypsy woman's rouged cheek a kiss.

The Face of Sappho

It appears as the face of Sappho
in my sleep
and then again in the morning
when the streets have been watered and swept,
before the hours of seagulls and heat.

She thinks there is
something I need to understand.
I lift to my lips cold water.
I dip my fingertips into the glass and
touch them to my eyes to stop them burning.

Her eyes, the eyes in her marble face,
have been chiseled to look wide open.
But what would she want to see
that she hasn't already seen
in twenty-four centuries?

At a cocktail party in her honor
the room rushes toward her.
Only I know
she is a broken set of prayer beads
spilled on the windowsill of a mosque.

How many years since she first came to me?
I remember moonlight and whippoorwills and a river
    valley.
And here I am old at last—
an accommodated man awakened
by the face of Sappho in a dream.

How the Day Began

Step by step the muezzin climbed
the hundred-and-one steps of his minaret
and assaulted the dark streets with the majesty of God.
His notes floated like jellyfish of the voice,
like the breasts of a woman
as she rides above a man,

then hardened when they struck the city's stone facades.
The street dogs roused. They took it into their heads
to rival the call to prayer with their howling.
That woke the crows, who grumbled in their leathery
    language
and flapped their wings like an ancient grudge
and woke the seagulls, who flocked and glided,
bringing whiteness to the city grey with dawn.

So now there were three colors:
Black of crows' wings stretching back to a time
before there was such a thing as time.
Gray of dawn and limestone and the lungs of old men
as they crept down city streets to pray in the mosque.
White of sea breeze and seagulls' ascension,
and white of the sheets where we woke.

Down in the mosque the old men had washed
away the night's blackness and were bending to their
    prayers,
stroking their beards and mumbling over their beads.
The dogs trotted along the pavement
and woke the sparrows, who told the air it was truly day.
A tomcat named Nero curled around a juniper bush
in a flowerpot, then grumped and stretched and yawned,
and watched with sleepy eyes the sparrows' doings.

And then what happened, darling?
You sidled alongside the length of my body
and we went back to sleep for a while.
From down in the street I heard two clangs of a trolley
    bell,
then the surge of shopfront shutters yanked open
and the steamy rush of a coffee machine.
You backed up onto me and warmed my hand on your
    breast.
What country were we in? Who was God? I couldn't
    remember.
The air smelled of everything.

A Saxophone Blew

A saxophone blew, windshield wipers
cleared the night's wetness,
turf smoke from cottage fires along the road
entered the car in sudden gusts
and I inhaled that peaty elixir
while the singer sang the marriage of Joan of Arc
with the flames of her martyrdom.
Yet I failed to recognize myself.

The saint's wedding dress hung in flounces
of wood-ash over the muddy countryside
like whitethorn blooming along hedges my headlights
illumined as I swung round bends in the road
singing, plunging headlong into my new life.

They Gambled for Your Clothes

Even with your head so wrong,
so eggshell-fragile,
nerve endings strobing out of control,
somehow here you are,
and for the moment nothing hurts.

Fight to stay awake and follow
her hands, skill of her fingers as she undoes
your bootlaces, works the boots off
your stiffened feet
and laves them—
silver bracelets on her wrists—
in the flinty stream
that runs through her property.

The dead skin of your ankles
shrieks morbidly,
blue and livid.

What a salad she has prepared for you—
what stainy walnuts,
what bitter curly greens veined
hallucinatory red.

She has found your hat somewhere in the road
and smoothed the dents away,
the bits of broken glass.
There your denim jacket is,
artfully mended, the blood washed out of it.

Amulets

Everything's all wrong today, my love.
I must have forgotten
to bow to the new moon
when she rose.

I'll go down on my hands and knees
and search in the gravel for five smooth stones,
each one different,
then knot them together
on a blood-red string
and hang them over our bed
to keep away nightmares.

Poor as my needle skills are,
I'll sew a jacket of red flannel
over a horseshoe
and keep it under the mattress,
tie a skeleton key to a bit of rope
to ward off the horrors.

Make me a pin cushion in the shape of a domino
marked with seven lucky dots.
Send down to the butcher shop
for a cow's head and a twisty
ram's-horn
to ward off lightning strikes.

Give me one of your dance pumps,
will you, darling,
from your party days?

I'll spray-paint it gold
and put it on the mantelpiece
to bring good luck down our chimney.

Look at it glistening there in the moonlight!

Cabbage

You planted cabbages to please me,
I know.
And there the last three or four of them clung
like pock-marked green moons in orbit
across the muddy sky of the garden slope.

We had to get out the hatchet
to chop the woody stem off the one I wanted.
And then I pulled off leaf after leaf,
each rubbery jacket bull's-eyed
like cigarette burns on an unfortunate table,
where slugs had tried to burrow in.

Before I brought it inside for a good scrub
I hacked off
half-a dozen leaves with my pocket knife
and flung them onto the compost heap,
flicking slugs off,
lacking the zeal even to deprive
them of their disgusting lives.
Autumn is here, and where
is the gardener's thoroughness
that would have been mine in March or May?

The essence of cabbage
as I chopped through its crunchy thickness
on the kitchen counter
was what the word October
smells like.
That pure white-and-greenness
that filled my head
with what grows and keeps on growing
was what I had needed all this
short and getting-shorter day.

II

Distance

Summer ends, the sky an unnameable
Dense blue. Lake depths. The effort to lift regret
Off your heart. Now the *pock* of a tennis ball,
Continuum of a motorboat across stillness,
Become an elegy. The bocce balls lie
Clumped on the bowling lawn as if they'll never
Budge again.
                    Feet cold under quilts at dawn.
Just enough goodbyes. The road rises
All morning past tarns dark as steeped tea, past
Shuttered cottages. At first, imaginings
Of what you might have left back there. Startle
Of scarlet in a maple.
                                Ahead, half-glimpsed,
A spiral cut into a mountainside.
How will you climb up where you need to go?

How to Get There

Take the old road out of town.
Follow it
to where crabgrass snaggles up
through cracks in the concrete
and the day turns chilly.
The sky you thought
roofed summer and a lake,
picnics and the breast stroke and an indigo
bunting poised on the finial of a jack pine
contains, instead, Canada as seen on weather radar—
flurries, and an air-blast
from shores where ice-floes crumble off a glacier.

Bear south when you spot
a pillar of cumulus stacked up in the heartbreaking
dense blue above a bungalow where
a man and a woman in canvas lawn chairs
sit with their backs turned to each other,
and a tow-headed kid
maneuvers a nicked yellow toy dump truck
through a canyon ten inches deep,
while black ants observe.

Don't stop. You can't stop. Keep going
until you reach an intersection
where thunder percusses the shuddering inner spaces of
   sky
and lightens from within
cloud-pockets going dove-grey and gun-metal blue—
past a '48 straight-eight Buick
and thumb-sucking and daydreams,
past words like destination, and hot and cold,
and shame and regret
and starry diadem and Old Town canoe.

Keep driving
through the gap that opens between two novice
    heartbeats.
Before decades, before skies, before the first summer,
before any knowledge of roads and weather.
Back to where you are an infant again, open-mouthed,
and the whole world lies in wait for your wondering eyes.

One Morning a Rose Blooms

and swallows glide atop heat-swells.
You gaze up at the black walnut tree
over the deck as if it would never alter.

But all at once the leaves have gone yellow.
Then one morning the tree is a bleak crown;
tweeds and flannels hang in your closet.

Another morning you are looking for your gloves
and the phone number
of the man you buy firewood from.

The deck has been cleared now and swept clean.
A crow tries to fly but the wind blows him sideways
in its relentlessness.

How good to have built a sanctuary
and put a roof on it—
painted it green and awakened a fire

at the heart of it to splinter the distances
between this room and the cold
miles of the galaxies.

Flowers, because everyone needs
the transport of flowers to take away
the marks made on the heart by treachery

and blandness and stupidity—
your own as much as others'.
That's what darkness is.

The sky goes blank for an afternoon
and a morning. Then it rains.
And then the snow starts to fall.

This is why you have brought a tree inside
and put lights on it
and filled your house with

fragrance and fire and food and
carols for Christmas morning:
Noel, Noel, Noel.

Watcher Over the Dead

in memoriam A.N.L., 1902–1995

I left the brandy and the flushed faces and the stories
  and tears at the wake,
recalling the time
we sat around the fire in his log house in Monteagle,
  drinking Old Weller's from silver julep cups,
and he insisted we read aloud
from a newspaper story that described him at seventy-
  five
as "barrel-chested and sexy."
He crowed when we got to that part.

Not even my old friends would have understood if I tried
  to tell them
how he anointed my house with fire
six hundred miles away on the night of the funeral
when a candle in his namesake my son Andrew's room
  burned out of control—
imperiling all but injuring no one.
But that hadn't happened yet, wasn't going
to happen till after his body went into the ground—
and I'm not sure if I have understood that mystery yet.

I left the wake and walked out under oak leaves and the
  round moon
along the top of the mountain to the chapel of St.
  Augustine.
It was three in the morning.
The hour struck, and that reverberation of bronze and
  stone
touched the depths at which his death was lodged in my
  being.

Up in the west wall the rose window glowed
rose-madder and scarlet and some blue I can't render.
The carpenter wasn't ready yet with the coffin lid
which the next day in our dark suits we took turns
shoveling the gravelly red dirt onto.
So only a cloth stretched over the open box standing on
    trestles that night.
I lifted it, and there was the man I had known.

His eyes were shut. His face clenched around some
    preoccupation
that made him seem not himself at all—
he who was arch and merry, and delighted in mimicry.

I touched his heavy hands with their ridged fingernails.
I touched his cheek—hard as plaster, colder than
    anything that lives.
Again the tower clockworks ground into motion.

Camille Monet on Her Deathbed

after the painting by Claude Monet

Camille has ventured out in a blizzard it seems.
Her husband has brushstroked her in in a hurry as she
        lies there dead.
What looks like a bridal veil rides up over her head,
the mouth open, showing the teeth.
The flared nostrils suggest hard breathing
        just past.

Of her, what do we know other
        than smudges of pigment—
a touch of bruised scarlet in the eye of the storm
where maybe she clutched a red kerchief in her agony.
Or could someone have given her flowers to hold?

And is that her right
hand, a claw roughed in on the coverlet—
        cobalt blue over the ice-slick of bedclothes?

Apparition from nightmare,
a white cloth tied up under her chin
        to lock her jaw shut,
her body in its dark nightdress cuts
—as in a dream I can't wake up from—
        underneath the fog of her surroundings
like a tugboat transgressing through the harbor.

First It Is Taken Away from Me

And now I am home again.
I can sit out in my pajama bottoms,
                        two cats sprawled
belly-down on the warm deckboards
                to converse with
the Saturday after Father's Day.
The air is saturated with moisture
as a rum cake is with rum.

Like a tourist, like a slow boater,
                like a firefly past the solstice,
I hover and scull and wobble
through these haunts and currents and air-pockets,
the day's emptiness
        radiant in the hollow of my spine.

Of the hospital I remember only:
Dry mouth, icy feet, rough dreams.
Nausea of waxed linoleum
down a hall the gurney ran along
                at scaresome speed.
The gabble of television sets,
and low voices leaking through half-closed doors.
The graph of the monitor repeated, repeated, repeated.

Burgundy velvet like the robe of a grand vizier,
the clematis blossoms like big sagging stars
                        or moonfish
soak light in and collapse it into their mystery.

The clematis plays Juliet on her balcony,
bosoming out into moonlight,
ripe with the desire to be known,
giving herself, wishing to taste and be
permeated by the world,
        as if she had never breathed air till now.

That's how it is with me,
                wing-shot and hampered as I am,
idly rubbing the IV tape marks off my arm.

Glimpse of a Traveller

A stranger with a Sunday to kill
Before flying out of Shannon,
He stands at the bar in the Old Ground Hotel
In jeans and a Savile Row jacket,
Drinking a black-and-tan,
Writing in a notebook he takes from his pocket.

He looks well against the background
Of dark walnut and stained glass.
Above bricky pouches, his eyes comprehend
The life that circulates just beneath the surface
Around him. Foam from his pint clings
To one of his moustache's lopsided wings,
But he takes no notice.

Surely there was a boy here once
With parents, schools, summer camps and crushes
And his own ways of destroying his innocence.
It's hard to tell what flinches
His handsome deadpan features mask.
Is he a ladies' man or a family man
Adrift? You'd have to ask—
If you ever lay eyes on him again.

A Love Story

He was an overage party boy,
handsome in a retro sort of way,
handy with a hip flask or a joint—
   a 60s throwback
who broke a lot of rules and glasses
and a heart or two, or so they say.
"Don't try to analyze fun, for fuck's sake,"
he told me late one night, slurring his s's.

She was a bit of a slapper—
if you know what I mean—
with her short black skirts in black taxis,
her cell phone and thirst for experience,
and a string of love-affairs with unsuitable men.
London was a dance,
   a party dress
that fell at her feet in a beautiful mess.

You could have knocked me over with a feather
when I saw them together in a dingy cafe
off the Fulham Road amidst the smell of damp wool
and a whiff of diesel off the street—
sitting there in full possession of each other,
her big diamond ring catching the light.
They looked like two saints from a medieval
manuscript, two mated birds of prey.

Something anarchic in their eyes had been tamed.
Two wildnesses had reached the pitch of their headlong
flight. They had been up all night
talking. I could no more have entered the space

they occupied than I could have stepped through the
      frame
into that illumination where they belonged
and I did not. So I turned and walked out
before they could notice.

They're living in the country now, or so I've heard,
with an apple orchard and a hive for bees.
They graze their sheep above a cloud
on a mountainside where they grow their own
veggies, make jam and live by the phases of the moon.
I picture them there gazing into each other's eyes
in that redeemed, unlisted place,
with a dog called Lucky and a cat named Grace.

My Guardian Angel

My guardian angel! I'd have to laugh
if you weren't so real.

Only you and my parents and my first wife and all
my unhappy girlfriends from years ago
and the seminarian I conned out of that 12-string,
and various other people
know all my character flaws.

Remember the time I left my body
freewheeling down the coast road
in my old Volkswagen?
Thanks for steering.
You're a mensch.

They must have let you listen in on
those embarrassing prayers I prayed
while our skiff
knocked against the hard waves
in a force-eight wind.
You met us at the dock on the mainland
with sandwiches and a flask of whiskey.

Arrival

Remember how knackered we were,
                how wobbly at the ankles—
burning ourselves out on the road,
             knocking on Heaven's door?
Exhaustion was part of our intoxication—
       exhaustion, repairs, Bob Dylan,
            uncertain breakfasts, highway miles.

We turned our wheels in toward the curb,
    detritus of the journey adrift around our feet,
and stumbled out of
        the truck heavy with our East Coast belongings,
onto the legendary streets of Denver,
    its sky streaked apple-green at dawn—

you in your sheepskin coat,
             me in my halo of anticipation,
the children loosed from their car-seat and crib
        blinking at arrival and
    brick storefront fantasias emerging from the darkness,
coalsmoke in our wintry nostrils.

    In our retinas, a sky adorned with clouds
        forever regrouped ahead of us.
Rubber-banded to the sun-visor,
            an interstate map of the US
   spanned the hemisphere's curve
           from Boston to the Rockies.

Sure, we could have made a
    more elegant appearance—
I could even have shaved off my road-stubble.
Yet here we were
        emerging from the tunnel of distance, a family.

Somehow you had entrusted your future
    to my hands on the wheel and my foot on the gas,
my skill with a screwdriver and socket-wrench and
    fountain pen,
            my blood in the veins of your babies.

Snowflakes & a Jazz Waltz

You have things to do, but the snow doesn't care.
As contemplation leads you
from window to window, the snow
accompanies you.
Whenever you glance up from the page, there it is—
layered, dense, constant.

It amplifies the volume of space
and gives you a way of telling time.

Eradication of emptiness, a specific against ennui,
it works, like truth, on a slant.

Its lightness
responds to gravity
by drift and evasion.
As you drive around town
it slackens and intensifies—
a sideways sizzle of dashes and dots.

While you circle the block, visualizing a parking place,
listening on tape to the cymbal-glide
and diminished chords of a jazz waltz
from forty years ago
when you were twenty,
a cash register rings

through the buzz and boozy hum of the Village
    Vanguard
one Sunday afternoon through cocktail chatter and
cigarette smoke exhaled
by people many of whom must now be dead.
Bill Evans is. Scott LaFaro is—
killed in a car crash
decades ago.

But not you. You drive
through the snow and the morning.
Snow drifts and ticks;
Bill Evans vamps,
and Scott LaFaro's fingers slap against the strings
of his standup bass
in time with the Honda's windshield wipers and
tires whirring over packed snow.

It snows while you go into the bank and buy euros
and it's snowing when you
come out again.

Snowflakes—white constellations
dissolving.
          Indelible
snowflakes
printing the book of your hours.

III

Big Doors

I have seen with my own eyes doors so massive,
two men would have been required
to push open just one of them.
Bronze, grating over stone sills, or made of wood
from trees now nearly extinct.

Many things never to be seen again!
The fury of cavalry attacking at full gallop.
Little clouds of steam rising
from horse droppings
on most of the world's streets once.

Rooms amber with lamplight
perched above those streets.
Pilgrimage routes smoky with torchlight
from barony to principality through forests
which stood as a dark uncut authority.

A story that begins "Once upon a time."
Messengers, brigands, heralds
in a world unmapped from village to village.
Legends and dark misinformation,
graveyards crowded with ghosts.

And when the rider from that story at last arrives,
gates open at midnight to receive him.
Two men, two men we will never know,
lean into the effort of
pushing open each big door.

In the Parking Lot of the Muffler Shop

for Gary Snyder

Between the muffler shop and the Shell station
three pines that survive where four were planted
on a strip of earth five feet across, forty long,
spill their seed cones out onto asphalt.
The pungency of eight stunted junipers
quickens the lunchtime air.

I kick indifferently among
the jetsam that has sedimented up
against the curb somebody
once painted white and then forgot about.
Dandelions take root in black sand
among filter tips, pine needles,
the snapped-off bottleneck from a longneck Bud,
rust and rubber of
manufactured parts that made cars go and stop,
things that appeased the snarl of engines
and spread the pollution out evenly.

Cool air smelling of tires and gear-box oil
exhales from the service bay of the muffler shop
as from a mountain cave.
Inside, the measured clank of heavy tools
applied with deliberation.

Three trees don't make a forest.
I sit in the shade of this reservation
between a white Cadillac and a red pine,
and a voice says to me:
Archaeologize the ordinary.
Sing songs about the late Machine Age.
Chronicle the in-between.

In the vacancy of noon,
sparrows twitter. At a distance, a phone rings.
Right here where they have spent the whole of their lives,
three pines stand.

Eclogue

Luminous days and straight-up skies.
Emergences and emanations.

This is the season for carrying water.
In an old zinc watering can.
A gallon at a time.

The season my white rosebush
    looks like Miss Havisham's wedding gown.

We breathe all summer long in
outdoor rooms with leafy walls,
rooms with trees forming their four corners,

    airy spaces the mind
        prunes from nature—
stanzas that don't reveal themselves in snow time.

Tiger lilies trumpet
    heat and dust and long days and forgetfulness.
The year, having leveled out at the solstice,
        tilts on its axis.

Istanbul: Meditations on Empire

The poem I wrote last night in my dream
disappears before breakfast.
Scraps of it blow by me
down thousand-year-old streets:
Centurions on the march,
columns of legions
with faces identically carved, spears at the ready.
And out in front of them, warrior emperors
with archangelic profiles and hawk-like zealots' eyes.
In winged boots of silver they strode,
crosses on their banners.
Seraphic script told their legends in Greek.

St. Gregory of Nyssa writes: *I wish to know*
the price of bread. The bread man answers,
"The Father is greater than the son." I ask whether my
bath is ready. My servant replies,
"The son has been made from nothing!"
In streets, markets, squares and crossroads,
they talk of nothing else.
When they deposed an emperor, they slit his tongue
and cut off his nose.

Plastic bottles, filter tips
and every other non-biodegradable thing
piles up around
rows of helmeted marble legions
stuck haphazardly in the mud
beside a bus stop and a mosque
after the archeologists left.
Among the huge peacock-eyes on fallen marble shafts
one row of soldiers has been cemented in upside down.

It's all use and re-use and refuse.
Bells from my dream hammer against
the cracked and buckled marble of Byzantium.
God rings the bells, earth rings the bells, the sky itself is
ringing.
The Holy Wisdom, the Great Church, is ringing out the
message.
For every bell there is a priest, and for every priest a
deacon.
To the left the emperor is singing, to the right the
patriarch,
and all the columns tremble with the thunder of the
chant,
while nomadic border-fighters, their eyes blood-enflamed,
muscle over the city walls
and their cannons blast gaps through which more fighters
pour.

Once Constantine's city was looted and ravished
for the customary three days
and the fires died down,
while stiffening corpses lay about the streets
and dogs fattened,
the Conqueror, in sky-blue boots,
wearing an enormous turban,
dismounted, sprinkling a handful of dust on his head,
and entered through one of the church's nine bronze doors,
quoting a melancholy distich in Persian—
something about a spider
spinning her web in the Palace of the Caesars
and an owl hooting from the towers
of a king whose name I don't remember.

Dome over dome over dome
gone the way the Venetians would go
with their glorious waterborne empire.
The polluted tides of history slosh up underneath it all—
the stone lion of St. Mark's propping up
an eroded tablet of Christ's gospel
at high tide
of bitter coffee and oil slicks and coal smoke
in any port in the Mediterranean
from Malta to Constantinople.

I make my way with a headache
and unsure feet down a steep street in Pera
where a dead-drunk woman in a cotton housedress
lies passed out on the sidewalk,
everyone just walking around her
as if she were a sack of garbage
here in this crossroad of empires.

Back in my hotel room I drink hot brandy
and read Graham Greene
while on CNN a new empire,
having neither the poetry and absolutism of the Turks,
nor the otherworldliness and willingness the Byzantines
        had
to cut out an enemy's tongue in the name of God,
moves into the deserts of Mesopotamia.
A general with a Great Plains accent
stands in front of an easel and points out Baghdad and
        Damascus.
All he knows of these cities
he learned from a map in the back of his Bible.

Hotel Room

In this room I laid out my prayer rug
and greeted the sun.
On the one-chair balcony I sat out
from dinner till late at night

and watched the domes of the great mosques
turn liquid with moonlight
as if filling up from within—
silver like the nightingale's tongue.

First the epic journey,
the last mad dash down a mountainside,
arriving hollow-eyed and sunburned,
then this room.

Ten

Call me Perfector of the Perfect Number,
knowing the world and beyond-the-world
through all ten senses,
my ear opening to the cries of a street vendor
and rain before sleep or sleeplessness.
Tires on a wet street,
the rapidity of fingers on a keyboard
like raindrops on wet glass.
The ten fingers that type
become the ten that touch your dangerous nipples
as they announce themselves
and now ten is me and I am ten as I write and
my breath quickens along with yours.

My fingers become the ten suras of the Holy Koran.
And I blaspheme again
by likening my ten toes to the Ten Commandments,
which are stepping stones
unto my feet even as I observe them and
disregard them and reinterpret them,
thus outraging the ten
states of the old Confederacy
plus Texas and one other
and my home state, Tennessee.

I thought I saw you at the bus stop today
but you are two continents away
and five time zones—
and those two continents are your breasts,
which my ten perfected fingers
receive even as you rise above
me and lean down to me
and take my wayward sloop,
which I nickname the Unifier,

into your harbor
and the waves of your accession
lap over me, and that sets me free to
ascend through the ten skies of Paradise,
veiled like the Prophet.

Here, let me dip my pen
into the waters of separation,
says the number ten.
Let me share my quintessence,
let my ten accompanying angels
draw me upward in their ten-cornered
net of ecstasy and divide my tenfold nature,
let them cut me with their ten swords
painlessly, and release me into the
decades and centuries of history
and into the decimals of language.
Strike ten bells, each with the power of ten decibels,

and when ten monks hear them ringing
let them name a *decanus* to govern themselves,
recalling the leaders of ten in the Roman legions,
who rest on their spears as uncouth
tribesmen come to barter,
leading mules down a mountain track,
each bearing a *decuria* of ten hides
as their unit of trade.
Let them decimate each other, if they must,
while I as Perfector of the Perfect Number
abdicate the world of essence
for the world of commerce and measurement.

Let somber Albanians in white skullcaps call me
    quindakia
and Bulgarians with resinated wine and garlic
on their breath call me *stotinka*
and carry me clinkingly in their goatskin purses.
I'll be dinars and tenners and ten-spots
for the world to spend.
Leave ten percent on the table for the
waiter to feed his ten children.

Soon enough I'll slide into this world again,
ears roaring with the waters of birth
at ten in the morning on the tenth day of the tenth
    month
as the midwife holds me up to the sunlight,
counting the ten perfect digits of my hands and feet.

Like One Who Is New in Paradise

for Elif Safak

It begins with a smell coming up out of the ground,
foul in origin but not unalluring.
An odor that rises from underground cisterns.

Then diesel exhaust and sea breeze and fresh-cut
lemons and cigarette smoke.
A marble threshold that has stayed
white and marbly for a thousand years.

Dust. The sun baking splayed fig leaves.
The perishability of a melon.
The heaviness of a life spent at physical labor.

Hundreds of years of burdened feet
have made the cracked mosaic pavement glow
like a river with morning mist.
The print of a foot evaporates from rained-on
horizontals of stone.

From that footprint come
alleyways and taxi racket and ships' horns,
Prayer is better than sleep at four AM, and mosquitoes,
and melismas of God's announced majesty.

And here I am like one who is new in paradise—
trying to speak the language I hear,
drinking from a fountain ostensibly dry.

Unmoored—
with a view through grapevines to a street
someone has hosed down and swept,
where children in blue
uniforms go on their way to school.

As Long As I Have These Saddlebags

As long as I have these saddlebags
I think I will be all right.
The sun in their weave, their wool stained
   like a stained-glass window,
their scorpion shapes and stylized camels
and cities with gates locked against marauders—
those clinched and vigilant symbols
doze like evolved watchdogs on my sofa.

One day I will lose this coin.
But as long as I have it,
I am walking the Street of the Fortunate
above the blue fabric, the silver scales of the sea—
through Cherries-that-Weigh-down-the-Bough Street,
on foot down the Street of the Little Holy Wisdom—

keeping in my pocket the coin that will
pay my way across
in a long wooden craft,
the boatman singing above the pulling oars.

My journeys
are slow marches
over mountains freckled with snow,
over black walnut trees that were cut down
to make my floors.

It's true I am kindling a fire today
on my own bricks,
not throwing together a rough blaze
with truck drivers and camel drivers and smugglers
stoking a water pipe on the dirt floor
of a caravansaray with gates standing open
to scavenger dogs gnawing bone-scraps, and wolves

and wind off the Hindu Kush.
I don't shiver with cold and the rain doesn't
needle my shoulders.
I don't have to favor my right knee as I climb
or wonder if my boots will fail me.

In the pilgrimage that is underway
I might not be among the trekkers.
But my fingers, like these saddlebags, are stained
    with the colors of the journey
and my hands smell of the currency of passage.
Praise God I am one of the travellers
as long as I have this coin in my pocket.